MW01132219

The Master Teacher

by

Dr. Norvel Hayes

Harrison House
Tulsa, Oklahoma

Unless otherwise indicated, all Scripture quotations are taken from the *King James Version* of the Bible.

14 13 12 11   7 6 5 4

The Master Teacher
ISBN 1-57794-093-8
Copyright © 1997 by Norvel Hayes
P.O. Box 1379
Cleveland, TN 37311

Published by Harrison House, Inc.
P. O. Box 35035
Tulsa, Oklahoma 74153

'You Will Do Greater Works'

The Holy Ghost is a great Teacher, and He will lead you personally into victory in every area in your life.

I want to share with you some things that have happened to me personally, things that He has taught me.

I haven't obeyed Him every time. But the Holy Ghost will warn you against things that He doesn't want you to get into, such as businesses. Or He'll warn you about people and their spirits. But if you disobey Him, you will go through some hard times.

Jesus said,

> **Verily, verily, I say unto you, he that believeth on me, the works that I do shall he do also, and greater works than these shall he do; because I go unto my Father.**
>
> **John 14:12**

You can do whatever you want to do in Jesus' name, if you use Scripture. If you don't, you can't do anything because Jesus is sitting on the right-hand side of the Father.

He said here in John 14:12 that He was going unto His Father. That's the reason you can do greater works than He did, because He's making intercession for you.

Jesus says we can do greater works, but we don't. And you know we don't. Why not? Because He had a greater amount of the power than we have. But why don't we have a greater amount of God's power in the church today and in individual lives today?

We don't pay the price to get God's power. It doesn't come cheaply.

The only reason you can't do any more than you're doing now is that you don't have enough power. You can do anything if you have God's power to do it. Jesus had a lot of God's power. He paid the price to get it.

The Holy Ghost who came from heaven in the form of a dove and rested upon Jesus when John the Baptist baptized Him, rested in Him, and taught Him. That same Holy Ghost lives in you today.

But just because the Spirit of God

lives in you is no sign that you'll have
the power to do those greater works.
You have to get Him to manifest
Himself. And the way you do that is to
praise God, spend time worshipping
God, and get scriptural in your believing. You may believe this or that, but it
may not bring any power because you
may be believing wrong.

Praying Scripture Creates Power

Check up on what you believe.
Make sure it's in line with God's Word,
and then the power comes. The power
always follows the Scripture and every
individual that believes the Scripture.

That's the reason God wants you to
have a chapter and verse when you
pray. Don't pray just to pray. Have a
chapter and verse for your foundation
when you pray, and stand on it. That
way you move the heart of God, and
He'll give your answer to you. God has
to approve of the way you're praying
and if you don't pray in Jesus' name
with Scripture, God doesn't approve of
your praying.

'Except the Lord Build the House...'

Jesus said you'll do greater works than these "...because I go unto my Father." Jesus loves you so much, He is going to make intercession for you — but not if you don't stand on Scripture when you pray.

That's the reason when you build a church, you'd better know it's God's will or it will be built in vain. The blessing of God on something is what makes it successful and a blessing. God has to approve of it. If He doesn't, stay away from it.

You may see a fellow doing a good work, but that's no sign you're supposed to do it. You're not a puppet. Don't try to copy somebody else. God wants to use you as an individual. He has a job for you to do. And you can find out what that job is if you'll just seek His face and pray. You can find your place in God.

I began to get hungry for the power and the glory. God began to deal with me about my need for His reality.

8

The Touch of God

You have to lay your education and money aside and come to God as a simple child and say, "Lord, use me." And He will. You may not like it; your friends may think you're nuts; but that's all right. You need the glory of God. Your body and your mind need to be saturated with the glory of God. We need a spiritual bath every once in a while.

Those who hunger and thirst after righteousness, they shall be filled. I can't go too long without praying where the power of God comes on you and you fall on your knees and cry and weep and just praise God. It's called "the touch of God." I just get on my knees and say, "Jesus, I'm hungry and I'm thirsty and I want to be filled with Your holy presence. Give it to me, Jesus. I want to drink from the fountain that flows from God." In a few days, here it will come. Glory to God!

Hunger and Thirst
After Righteousness

The Bible says you have to get hungry for God. Are you hungry? If you haven't been filled lately, you're not hungry enough. If you haven't drunk lately, you're not thirsty enough. Oh, get hungry and thirsty after God, after righteousness, and you shall be filled. When you get hungry and thirsty, the Greater One in you will begin to manifest Himself. He'll teach you what God wants you to have. You won't make any mistakes because He'll teach you the truth.

> **And whatsoever ye shall ask in my name, that will I do, that the Father may be glorified in the Son.**
>
> **If ye shall ask any thing in my name, I will do it.**
>
> **John 14:13,14**

Glory to God forevermore. Jesus said, "If...." He didn't say *you would*, He said, "*If* you would ask..."

> **If ye love me, keep my commandments.**
>
> **And I will pray the Father, that he shall give you another Comforter, that he may abide with you forever.**
>
> **John 14:15,16**

Clean Vessels for the Holy Spirit

The Holy Ghost will never leave you or forsake you. He will live in you, and He will lead and teach you and guide you into all truth. He will never leave you or forsake you as long as you will stay out of sin.

Paul says in his writings that the Greater One, the great Comforter, the Holy Ghost will not live in an unclean vessel. But Jesus plainly said, "If you love Me, keep My commandments." If you don't, that's a sign that you don't love Him.

In other words, Jesus said, "Don't say that you love Me and go out and commit sin because if you do, you're a liar. If you loved Me, you wouldn't turn your body and your life over to sin."

Jesus loves your body. He loves every part about you. Don't try to live a double life. Just give up sin, because it's no good anyway. It's not ever going to do anything for you except cause you heartaches and trouble and torment. You're never going to get anything out of telling a lie or committing adultery.

11

The Holy Spirit Within

You can drive yourself crazy by not listening to the Holy Ghost. He is the great Teacher within you. He will teach you how to live. Billy Graham says the biggest problem in American today is that American people don't know how to live.

When anything bad happens to you, resist the devil. Just say, "I resist you, in Jesus' name!" Jesus said that if you'll do that, the devil will flee from you; he will start running away from you.

So don't be afraid of the devil. When you live your life clean, he's already defeated. Jesus defeated him. But you have to use Jesus' name and stand boldly with authority. Devils have to obey you; they have no choice.

But you have to *know* that. You can't play religious games and get the job done. But you can take authority over the devil the same as anybody else can if you'll just go ahead and *do it*.

And I will pray the Father, and he shall give you another Comforter, that he may abide with you for ever....

John 14:16

When that Comforter comes, He will teach you the truth of the gospel of the Lord Jesus Christ. You talk about success — you'll have success if you listen to the Greater One inside you. Jesus said, "Even the Spirit of truth; whom the world cannot receive." No, the world can't receive Him. You have to bow down before Him and repent of your dumb sins and ask Him to come into your life. *Then* He will come into your heart and take over your life if you'll let Him. Surrender yourself to him, and the Spirit of God, the Spirit of truth, will lead you into the life that Jesus wants you to live. "Because it seeth him not." That's the reason the world can't understand or receive Him because it seeth Him not.

> ...neither knoweth him: but ye know him; for he dwelleth with you, and shall be in you.
>
> I will not leave you comfortless: I will come to you.
>
> Yet a little while, and the world seeth me no more; but ye see me: because I live, ye shall live also.

**At that day ye shall know
that I am in my Father, and ye
in me, and I in you.**

**He that hath my command-
ments, and keepeth them, he it
is that loveth me: and he that
loveth me shall be loved of my
Father, and I will love him, and
will manifest myself to him.**

John 14:17-21

When Jesus said, "I will manifest
myself to him," He meant to anybody. I
had a man ask me one time, "What
about me? How can I get God to manifest Himself to me?"

How Do I Find God?

I spoke in a church in Atlanta,
Georgia, one Sunday and was getting
ready to leave on Monday morning for
my office in Tennessee when the pastor
came in and said, "Brother Norvel,
there's a very successful businessman
here in town who wants to take us both
to lunch."

I said, "Do you think he just wants
to talk to me, or do you think it's God?"

"I believe it's God; the man sound-

14

ed desperate. He heard you speak in the service yesterday morning and said that God sent him there."

As the man was driving us to lunch, he just pulled his car over to the side of the road. I was in the front, and the pastor was in the back.

The man said to me, "Mr. Hayes, I'm thoroughly convinced that you know God. I never heard anybody talk like you. God took me to that church yesterday morning. Nearly every word you said blasted my life, hit me right in the face. My understanding was opened up. In fact, I told God a few weeks ago, 'God, if You're real, and I knew I could find You someplace, I'd go across the country if I knew You'd be there when I arrived.'"

He asked, "How do you find God? I believe that you've found Him and know Him personally. But that doesn't help me. I want to find Him for myself. How do I find God for myself?"

I said, "You find him through faith and believing. By the grace of God and through your faith, believing that He's real, and confessing your sins — that's the way you find Him."

"I want Him to manifest Himself to me. I want to *know* that He is real."

I told him "Jesus said, 'I will love him and will manifest myself to him.' God will manifest Himself to you when you please Him, when you get hungry enough."

He said, "I'm not just hungry, I'm desperate!"

I said, "I'll pray with you before we leave you today."

A Holy Spirit Suggestion

So we went to lunch and then came back and sat in the front of his business. As I began to pray for him, the Spirit of God, the great Teacher on the inside of me, told me, "Take him to the Washington, D.C. convention of the Full Gospel Businessmen. (I had planned to go to the one in Tampa, Florida, on that same day.)

"Sir," I said, "God just dealt with me to take you to Washington, D.C. and spend three days with you at the Full Gospel Businessmen's Convention. Will you go?"

16

"If I could spend three days and nights with you, asking you questions and getting you to pray for me, I would go anywhere in the world."

I gave him the dates and told him we would meet on Thursday and stay until Sunday in the greater Hotel Hilton. Later I called him and asked, "What time does your plane get in, Bob?" Mine gets in at 11:07."

He said, "I get in there at 11:07."

I said, "Thank You, Jesus."

We met at the luggage counter and were able to catch the first meeting at 2:30 that afternoon. Kathryn Kuhlman was speaking, and the place was packed with about three thousand people. We couldn't sit together, but a friend of mine got Bob a seat near the front. I didn't get to see him any more until we met in the room afterward. He came in and said, "My, my. I am more confused than ever."

"Why?" I said.

He said, "You know, I believe some of those people actually got healed! She called a woman out and said the woman

17

had cancer. She prayed for her and she fell on me."

I said, "Thank You, Jesus."

He said, "I helped lift her up. You know, I believe she got healed."

Paying the Price

I said, "Well, sure, she probably did get healed. Jesus heals people, Bob, if you believe Him, if you trust Him. He spent about half or two-thirds of His ministry all the way through the New Testament healing people: cripples, blind people, and all kinds of diseases. Leprosy on people's faces — He'd pray and it would just disappear. He had the power, but He paid the price to get it. He'd pray in the mountains for a day or two or all night long. He'd come back and the disciples would be asleep.

The Demon-Possessed Boy

Jesus would say, "Fellows, can you help me pray just one night?" That's the reason the disciples couldn't cast the demon out of the demon-possessed boy when the father brought his son to them. The Bible doesn't say they "*wouldn't* cast it out." They tried to, but it wouldn't go.

18

So they took the boy to Jesus, and Jesus cast the thing out of him.

Jesus told the father, "Bring him here." When the boy started coming toward Jesus, that thing attacked the boy again and made him take a fit. And I can imagine Jesus saying, "My, my, how old was this child when this thing came into him?"

All Things Are Possible To Him that Believeth

The father said, "It's been in him, Sir, ever since he was just a little child." (Remember what I told you earlier about a little child?) Jesus said, "All things are possible to him that believeth." And the father said, "I believe, I believe, Sir; help my unbelief. If You can do anything for us, please, help my child."

If you have lived with a demon-possessed person for years, I guess you might have a certain amount of wondering. You might try to believe but not know whether you can or not.

Why Couldn't We Do That?

Jesus just cast the evil thing out.

19

And the little boy fell over as if he was dead. Jesus said, "No, he's not dead." And he got up healed. The disciples came to Jesus and said, "Why couldn't we do that? We prayed for him, but nothing happened."

Jesus said, "First of all, because of your unbelief. Besides that, this kind only comes out by fasting and by praying."

Do you know what Jesus was telling them? "Remember those nights that I would go to the mountains and pray all night to the Father, before the throne of God where all the power is? I would come back, and you fellows would be asleep."

The Power of the Holy Spirit

Jesus didn't get the power just because He was the Son of God. Jesus did not operate on the earth in His ministry on what He inherited as God. That would mean that nobody else could have what He had. He operated by the power of the Holy Spirit of God, the same Spirit that lives in you if you've been born again. If you know Jesus as your personal Savior, then you can have the same power Jesus had, by faith. Just repent of your sins, ask Him to come in, and accept it by faith. "Through grace *by faith* are you saved."

Bob said, "Yeah, I believe that power was there and that it healed some of those people. But, Norvel, what about me? I want to find God for myself."

I said, "Well, you can find Him, Bob. Don't worry about it."

Early the next morning, God gave me a Scripture for him. I read it to him, and here he started up again.

"When am I going to find Him for myself? I want to find Him. What about me?"

I said, "Bob, you're going to find Him, just keep seeking Him and you'll find Him."

Testimony in the Ballroom

Once a year we have a breakfast at the Hilton Hotel and invite all the executives from the White House, the senators and the governors, diplomats from other nations visiting the White House, and the White House staff. I took Bob to that breakfast. Among those at my table was an ambassador from Africa and a senator from Tennessee. We were visiting, and then one of the largest car dealers in the country got up to say a few words for God. Next a professional baseball player testified about Jesus. A senator also spoke.

We were just minding our own business when they invited my friend to get up and say a few words for Jesus.

Every time my friend gets up — not part of the time, but *every time* he gets up, the glory falls on him, surging through his mortal body all over him. He got up and began to talk about Jesus and how Jesus saved him. Then he said, "I feel the glory coming on. It's crawling under my skin." And he started jumping up and down behind the pulpit, turning circles up and down — right in front of the governors and the senators. He couldn't have cared less who he was in front of.

He had been an old-fashioned preacher for years. He had accumulated a lot of money, about a million dollars, as a salesman and a good businessman, and he had lost every dime.

They came and repossessed his car. He owed about a million and a half dollars. He began to pray. He went from a Cadillac to hitchhiking. But he kept making a radio broadcast from Cincinnati, Ohio. He kept on preaching right in the midst of all of it.

"Better take bankruptcy; you're a million and a half dollars in debt." His friends told him.

But he said, "I know the God in whom I serve." And he kept on preaching. God began to move in his life because the great Teacher who lives inside of him began to teach him how to get out of that situation. He put his trust in Jesus and the great Teacher began to teach him how to pay off a million and a half dollars when he didn't have a dime. Meanwhile, all of his friends turned against him. (You can have all kinds of friends as long as you have money.)

So many people live in the world of dollar marks. Money talks in this country. But my friend came out of that completely — paid off all of it and was worth more than a million dollars. He had a fantastic testimony.

God Arrives

When the glory began to come over my friend, I looked over to Bob, and the holy presence of Almighty God began to move in that fancy ballroom; it just moved in over the congregation. Bob's mouth was quivering, and the skin on his face was jumping, and the tears were streaming down his cheeks. Bob was looking straight at my friend and the great Teacher in me, the Holy Ghost, said, "Go over and put your arm around Bob."

I walked over and put my arm around Bob. By that time everybody was standing up. The Lord just gave me the words, "Now, Bob, you've been wanting to find God. Would you be willing right in this fancy ballroom, with the great chandeliers and the governors and senators sitting here, to hit the floor on your knees this minute and cry out to God and ask Him to forgive you for your sins?"

He said, "Y-yeah."

I said, "Hit the floor, then; I'll go with you." We hit the floor about the same time on our knees. I had my hand on his back and said, "Repent, Bob, repent of those sins. Tell him you're sorry. Ask Him to come into your heart."

He cried out, "Jesus, I'm sorry for my sins!" and started crying and weeping. God moved on him so strongly, he couldn't even talk any more. When Bob said, "Jesus, come into my life, Lord," God hit him. For two days and two nights he had asked me, "When am I going to find Him, Norvel?" And now he was down on the floor on his knees, just crying and weeping. I said, "Bob, that's Him. You've found Him!"

"Y-yeah." But he couldn't stop crying. He got his handkerchief out and tried to wipe the tears, but couldn't for crying. Fifteen minutes later he was still crying. God moved on him. Talk about beautiful!

Bob cried for a day and a half. He said to me, "I found Him. It feels so good. Norvel, will it ever go away?"

I said, "He won't ever leave you or forsake you."

Bob called his wife up. He said,

"Honey, come up here; I've found Him." She said, "Found what?" He said, "I've found Him."

The next day, Bob was afraid to go home; he said, "I'm afraid I'll lose this. When I get off the plane and start toward my house, will I lose this? My children will think I'm nuts. My family will think I'm crazy."

I said, "Well, you are. You *are* nuts as far as the world is concerned. You're in the bunch of peculiar people, Bob. The people in the world won't understand you any more. But Jesus will."

A few weeks after that, he met me at the airport. There was a guy there about half drunk, and I was just coming off the plane. I just pitched my clothes bag on the floor, pulled the drunk out of the traffic, back over against the wall, and said, "I break your power, Satan, in Jesus' name; come out of this man!"

Bob said, "I've got to talk to you. Something is about to drive me crazy. Norvel, how do you ever get enough nerve to pray for somebody in the public like that?"

I said, "You don't pay any attention to the people. You look on the fellow." Later a woman called where I was staying to hold a meeting and she said, "Tell Brother Norvel to come over to my house; my kid is out of his mind. He's got a fever and is hot all over and talking out of his head. I'm afraid he's going to die."

I asked Bob if he wanted to take me. He said he would and that he knew where she lived. We went over there and the little kid was lying on the couch. I said, "Fever, I break your power in Jesus name. Come off that child in the name of the Lord Jesus Christ. I command you to turn that child loose, you thief. You're not going to steal this child. I break your power, and I command all the fever to leave this house in Jesus' name!"

At that moment, the child broke out in a sweat. The fever left; he batted his eyes and said, "Mama? Mama." I said, "He's healed. The peace of the Lord is here. He's completely healed. Go play, son."

27

The Greater One Inside

I said, "Now, Ma'am, you could have done that if you'd wanted to. The devil will obey you if you'll break his power. But you have to let the Greater One who lives inside you teach you all the truth, teach you in line with the Scripture. He'll teach you how to do these things if you'll let Him. But when He does, you have to obey."

And Bob said, "Norvel, do you mind if I follow you around for a while? Maybe I'd learn how to pray."

I said, "Feel free if you can take time off from your business; follow me around. Come to church this week and you'll learn a lot." He came. And he did learn a lot.

In fact, if you don't know much, you can learn a lot in one service. The Holy Ghost will teach you if you'll let Him.

He Will Teach You ALL THINGS

Judas saith unto him, not Iscariot, Lord, how is it that thou wilt manifest thyself unto us, and not unto the world?

Jesus answered and said

unto him, If a man love me, he will keep my words: and my Father will love him, and we will come unto him, and make our abode with him.

He that loveth me not keepeth not my sayings: and the word which ye hear is not mine, but the Father's which sent me.

These things have I spoken unto you, being yet present with you.

But the Comforter, which is the Holy Ghost, whom the Father will send in my name, he shall teach you all things....

John 14:22-26

God spells it t-h-i-n-g-s: "teach you all *things*."

I gave you the testimony about Bob who asked, "How do I find God?" God wanted him to go to Washington, D.C. Why? I don't know why. If you want to know, ask God. There's no use in questioning God. God told me to take him to Washington, D.C. for three days during that convention. He really found God.

Jesus said, "I will manifest myself to you." And his whole family changed.

A Daughter Out of Darkness

The Holy Ghost says He will teach you *all* things, not part of them, *all* things. The Holy Ghost, the great Teacher, taught me how to get my daughter out of darkness and back into the family of God. I thought I knew how because I was already teaching the Bible for Him. I thought I knew how, but the Holy Ghost let me know that I was wavering in my faith, and He said, "It will work because the Bible says it will work. Now get your faith straightened out. Your faith is strong enough to get her back into the family of God. But it's being applied wrong."

So I took inventory of what I was doing, of my approach to that child, and I found out I came up short of the Bible. God doesn't work in any way except the Bible way. I came up short of the love of God for my own child. If you had told me, I wouldn't have believed it, but the Holy Ghost told me. So I got my thinking straightened out. I said, "That's right. I see it, Lord. But Jesus, I didn't mean to." You see, you can not intend to do some things and still do them wrong.

I did what the Holy Ghost, the great Teacher told me to do for another year, and my daughter still wouldn't give in. But that didn't make any difference. What does that have to do with it? God sent an angel into her room one night, and she wound up seeking God's face. That angel scared her half to death. That's when she came back to God.

If you are born again, the Holy Spirit lives inside you. He is the master Teacher. And He wants to work with you so you can live by His power and begin to do those greater works that Jesus said you would do!

Books by Norvel Hayes

How to Live and Not Die
The Winds of God Bring Revival
God's Power Through
the Laying on of Hands
How to Triumph Over Sickness
Putting Your Angels to Work
Endued With Power
Financial Dominion
The Healing Handbook
The Blessing of Obedience
Stand in the Gap for Your Children
How to Get Your Prayers Answered
Number One Way To Fight the Devil
Why You Should Speak in Tongues

Available from your local
bookstore or from:

HARRISON HOUSE
P.O. Box 35035
Tulsa, OK 74153